loreen

She's The One

The Illustrated Biography

Carolyn McHugh

sona BOOKS

© Danann Media Publishing Limited 2023

First published in the UK 2023 by Sona Books an imprint of Danann Media Publishing Ltd.

WARNING: For private domestic use only, any unauthorised Copying, hiring, lending or public performance of this book is illegal.

CAT NO: SON0585

Photography courtesy of

Alamy images:

- Alejandra Espaliat
- Charlie J Ercilla
- DPA picture alliance archive
- Jeppe Gustafsson
- Patrick van Katwijk
- Roger Tillberg
- Sipa US
- TT News Agency
- WENN Rights Ltd
- ZUMA Press, Inc.

Getty images:

- Dominic Lipinsk
- Eduardo Parra/WireImage
- Frank Hoensch/Redferns
- Jeff Spicer
- John Phillips
- Joseph Okpako/WireImage
- Luca Teuchmann
- Nils Petter Nilsson
- Pablo Blazquez Dominguez
- Patricia J. Garcinuno/Redferns
- Photo by Thomas Niedermueller
- Ragnar Singsaas
- Shane Anthony Sinclai

Wikimedia Commons images:

- Albin Olsson
- Anders Henrikson
- Bengt Nyman
- Cassiopeija
- David Urdinguio
- Frankie Fouganthin
- Frankie Fouganthin
- Gulustan
- Jan Ainali
- Jonatan Svensson Glad
- Loreen Sjmanj
- Manfred Werner
- Mattias Olsson
- possan

Book layout & design Darren Grice at Ctrl-d
Copy editors: Tom O'Neill / Juliette O'Neill

All rights reserved. No Part of this title may be reproduced or transmitted in any material form (including photocopying or storing it in any medium by electronic means and whether or not transiently or incidentally to some other use of this publication) without the written permission of the copyright owner, except in accordance with the provisions of the Copyright, Designs and Patents Act 1988.Applications for the copyright owner's written permission should be addressed to the publisher.

This is an independent publication and it is unofficial and unauthorised and as such has no connection with the artist or artists featured, their management or any other organisation connected in any way whatsoever with the artist or artists featured in the book.

Made in EU.
ISBN: 978-1-915343-43-7

contents

early days 8

swedish idol 20

melodifestivalen 28

euphoria 38

heal 50

trying something new 58

making a statement 66

more music at last 74

raising the roof 82

tattoo 94

we got the power 110

i'm in it with you 114

long live queen loreen 118

discography 124

early days

Free-spirited and authentic, powerful and spiritual – there is no one quite like Sweden's Eurovision sensation, singer and music producer, Loreen.

That's possibly because not many artists of her standing have a nomadic heritage like hers. Loreen can trace her roots a mere one generation back to the Berber population of the Atlas Mountains in Morocco.

Berbers are native North Africans, famous for farming sheep, cattle, and goats, sometimes in one place, but very often moving around in the tough conditions of the Sahara Desert. They describe themselves as a 'free people' and their 4,000-year-old culture includes a strong tradition of singing and storytelling, using distinctive music and dances – remind you of anyone?

Loreen was born as Lorine Zineb Nora Talhaoui on 16 October 1983 in Stockholm where her Moroccan Berber parents had made their home after moving to Sweden in 1981. Her mother Choumicha was just 16, having fled her homeland two years earlier to escape the prospect of a forced marriage to an older man.

Atlas Mountains and Berber culture

The Atlas Mountain range in North Africa runs through Morocco, Algeria, and Tunisia for some 2,500 kilometres. Its highest peak is Toubkal in Morocco. The mountains are the traditional home of Berber people – descendants of the pre-Arab inhabitants of North Africa – who make up more than three fifths of the population of Morocco. Much of the architecture, crafts and clothing tourists associate with Morocco comes from the distinctive Berber culture.

early days 9

early days

Loreen feels very connected to her Moroccan heritage, believing her own strength and energy comes from this Berber lineage. She attributes her strong sense of conviction and self-belief to the fact that she is descended from a long line of strong, independent and courageous women on her mother's side, who fought for rights and freedom against the odds.

'All of the women, especially on my mother's side, are really powerful women, that have fought for their freedom and their liberty,' Loreen told *Scandinavian Vogue*. 'I've seen my mother still fighting for that.'

As well as witnessing her mother's struggle to provide for her family and make a life in a new country, Loreen discovered that her grandmother and great-grandmother were equally spirited, similarly rejecting the lives they were expected to lead. She tells a story in many interviews that her great-grandmother, who was reportedly very beautiful, was expected to remarry after she was widowed with two young children. But, vehemently against the idea, Loreen's great-grandmother escaped to Algeria where she had some family, leaving everything behind apart from her two children. From then until her dying day she dressed as a man, in a turban and kaftan, to cover herself up and avoid detection, opening and running a shop so that she could provide for her family without the need of a husband's support.

Such a strong sense of self-preservation evidently runs deep in the women of the family, so that Choumicha similarly found the strength to move away when she was also faced with an arranged marriage.

But having made it to Sweden she found that her new life in a foreign land still had its difficulties, particularly for a teenage mother. Speaking in the Swedish documentary *Livet enligt Loreen* (Life According to Loreen) Choumicha told Loreen, 'You were the first girl I was given. I was a child myself. But from that moment on I was not a child anymore. I had to be a mother.'

Loreen performs on stage during The Eurovision Song Contest 2013 Grand Final at Malmö Arena on May 18, 2013 in Malmö, Sweden

> *'We were a team', replied Loreen. 'I was chief of the siblings. When you were out I was the one who handled the house. We looked out for one another.'*

Certainly Loreen took on huge responsibilities as a child because within six years she gained five younger siblings. Her parents then divorced so it became little Loreen and her mother against the world. Although still a child herself, Loreen would collect her brothers and sisters from school and take care of them, including cooking and cleaning, when her mother was out working. There was no question – it was simply natural that Loreen and her mother would help each other.

'We had no other family in Sweden,' Loreen said in an interview with UK newspaper *The Guardian*. 'I had to grow up pretty fast. There are so many things I didn't understand because I was raised by a child myself…. The beautiful thing when you're raised by a young person is that it's hard to be judgmental because nobody's taught you how, you know?'

The household was poor but happy, and – as Loreen describes it, 'a riot – as it is in a Moroccan home. We were so many siblings, with music always playing. So I needed time by myself, and I got that.'

Her refuge became the family's bathroom, where she would lock herself away and sing. Always mindful that her eldest daughter needed this time to express herself Choumicha would tell the other children to leave Loreen in peace – and sometimes Loreen enjoyed hours alone to experiment with the bathroom acoustics.

'Singing was a way of healing for me as a child,' Loreen said. And her voice became her sanctuary.

Because she spent so much time 'in charge' at home she found it hard to follow any rules herself, which became a problem during her school years. 'No one could control me as I was head of the house,' she said. 'I was an authority, according to myself. I had responsibility and was the same character at school - demanding respect. I'm the same today – finding it difficult to follow rules.'

Her mother agrees, saying, 'Loreen wants to be in control of what she does. No one can control her, and she doesn't let the fear take over. For that I am proud of Loreen.'

But as a child it's not so easy to forge your own path. Schools have rules and regulations, neither of which sat well with Loreen. Coupled with that, her responsibilities at home marked her out as 'different'. 'No-one understood me,' she said. 'And because you are different you become a target.'

So here again she would escape to somewhere she could sing – this time she found the church in the school grounds. 'I would skip lessons and go there and sing because I liked the acoustics, like my bathroom at home!'

By now the family had moved 100km east of Stockholm out to Västerås, on the banks of Lake Mälaren. Loreen attended the Önstaskolan primary school and the Wenströmska Gymnasiet.

Things began to settle down by the time Loreen was a teenager at Wenströmska, largely because her mother had married again to a man Loreen liked: 'My mother was all about surviving. My stepfather was more like, "Maybe we should just calm down a little bit. Relax, enjoy the small moments, this connection, here. Everything doesn't have to be a struggle." I think he taught us how to show love'.

So, freed up from many of her 'parental' responsibilities by her new stepfather, Loreen began to settle down at Wenströmska where she enjoyed singing with music teacher Deborah Henriksson. Deborah came to have a great influence on young Loreen, recognising her talent and nagging her to use it.

'Not only did she have a good voice, but even then she interpreted the music she performed. In addition, she had charisma and drive and was completely herself", says Deborah. Although Loreen would often prefer R&B songs in those days, Deborah does have fond memories of providing piano accompaniment when Loreen sweetly sang **Over the Rainbow** from the musical The Wizard of Oz, during a school concert.

Loreen performs at 'The Dome 63' music show at the Forum Ludwigsburg on August 29, 2012 in Ludwigsburg, Germany

early days | 15

loreen *She's The One*

Loreen performs at Stockholm Pride 2012 on August 3, 2012 in Stockholm, Sweden

But although other people were already noticing that her singing abilities were exceptional, Loreen herself was becoming frustrated and angry at her perceived lack of progress – comparing herself unfavourably to stars such as Whitney Houston and Celine Dion. 'At the time I didn't understand that they were women, and I was a girl,' she said. 'Their vocal cords had matured where mine had not.'

But still tucked away in the bathroom at home she would persevere and practise, belting out massive songs like *My Heart Will Go On* from the movie *Titanic*. Her voice was so powerful even then that her mother bought earplugs for the rest of the family so that they wouldn't be disturbed when they were sleeping. She said it was no reflection on her daughter's voice!

Although Loreen often thought she might like to become a singer, a professional career in music was never really on the cards until one summer when the family went to visit her grandmother in Morocco.

Speaking in her native Berber, her grandmother wisely told her she had '… a gift that is not only meant for you, but one that can create great change'.

Suddenly everything fell into place for Loreen. She had always had a strong feeling that she wanted to help other people, particularly children, so much so that she had also briefly considered becoming a doctor.

But now her grandmother's words helped her to envisage a future in which she could sing and use any resulting influence to do good in the world.

Less than a year after that holiday she took her first steps towards a professional career by appearing on television in the first season of Sweden's Idol talent contest.

early days | 19

swedish idol

So with her grandmother's words ringing in her ears, a 20-year-old Loreen took her first tentative steps towards a professional career by appearing on the first series of the tv talent show *Swedish Idol* which sought to find the best singer in the country. She was encouraged by her sister who persuaded her to enter. 'My sister came up to me, and she's like, 'I want you to be on *Idol*,' and I'm like, '*** that!, Loreen told Sveriges Radio. 'But she made me somehow.'

Then, speaking more seriously, Loreen said that suddenly the idea had made sense to her. 'It was very spiritual. It happens once you say it, and once you feel it. Like, this is what I'm going to do, and you don't even have to know how.'

So in early 2004 Loreen joined the queue of hopefuls at the Stockholm auditions. Competing as Loren Talhaoui, auditionee number 4647, Loreen sang one of her favourite songs, *If I Ain't Got You* by Alicia Keys, a cappella. She stood before the four-strong *Idol* judging panel comprising voice coach Kishti Tomita, producer Daniel Breitholtz, talent scout Peter Swartling and producer, musician and disc jockey, Claes af Geijerstam.

It was a 'yes' from them so she advanced to the live semi-finals that September. There were five televised heats, each with eight contestants, two of whom would go through each week to the live finals, decided by a public vote.

At first Loreen just missed out on a place in the finals, having come third in her semi-final heat. But in the best traditions of reality television she got her 'second chance' when she was brought back into the competition as the wildcard 'judges' choice'. Having previously praised her 'cool tone, cool presence, and skillfulness', the judges made a wise choice as she went on to storm the first live final show. Its theme was 'My Idol' and again Loreen chose Alicia Keys' *If I Ain't Got You* which she had performed at her audition. But this time her performance was fully produced and orchestrated. She was on her way.

Many things about her were obviously different in those days. At 20, with short curly hair and a selection of girl next door costumes, she was yet to hit upon the cool expressive style for which she is famous today. But there was already no mistaking her impressive vocals and undeniable stage presence. Her ability to convey raw emotions through her singing resonated deeply with the viewers, establishing a strong connection that would later become her trademark.

As she advanced through the competition she was gaining confidence all the time and generally gained enough viewer votes to be 'safe' most weeks. But her time in the competition ended in the week eight show, despite her having given fantastic renditions of 1983 hits *Every Breath You Take* by The Police and *Thriller* by Michael Jackson for the theme 'My Birth Year'.

But by then anyway the competition had served its purpose. She had got her break, become known to the Swedish public, come fourth out of thousands of hopefuls and been the last woman standing, just two shows from the end of the series. She recognised these achievements immediately and dismissed the sad expressions and words of consolation from hosts David Hellenius and Peter Magnusson, telling them instead to smile and not be sad. 'I've had the time of my life', she said. 'Getting to do all this was more than I ever expected. And coming fourth is good, right?!'

As she knew, the experience of performing live before the nation was great training and she had learned a great deal, including breath control, microphone technique and how to work with multiple cameras.

She also received lots of advice from the judges who were all seasoned professionals from the music industry. 'You are one of my favourites in this competition,' said Daniel Breitholtz, which was praise indeed from such a renowned producer who had worked with many big stars including Whitney Houston. 'You are such a great talent - one of the best singers in the competition', agreed Peter Swartling.

swedish idol | 23

Loreen performs 'Euphoria' on stage at Cafe 40 on July 7, 2012 in Madrid, Spain

Yet despite all the acclaim, experience, and publicity she had gained from *Idol*, she was unsure about her next steps. When asked if she would be continuing with music she said, 'I don't know, we'll see.'

Her mysterious reply was because although her experience on *Idol* had undoubtedly helped to hone her talents, it had also highlighted an issue around being a woman in the modern music industry where behind the scenes are whole teams of people with a 'say' in your performance. She has since said that she found it 'painful' to be judged.

"All of a sudden, I had all these people telling me I'm not singing it right, and it confused me,' Loreen told Sverige Radio afterwards. It turned out that the whole *Idol* experience had been quite a challenge for her - a young woman who had largely performed instinctively until then.

But rather than be intimidated by her lack of industry knowledge at the time, Loreen decided to tackle the issue head on.

'When something is that challenging, you either back out or you say, "I'm going to learn this, and then I'll be in control",' she said. And that is what she did. After releasing one single post-*Idol*, *The Snake* with Swedish music duo Rob 'n' Raz in 2005, she took a hiatus - something that was to be a bit of a pattern moving forward. There was some music after *Idol*, and a little presenting work, but mostly Loreen began to work behind the cameras as a segment producer and director for SVT show *Frufritt*, and also for commercial channels TV3 and TV4. She taught herself film techniques including editing and lighting, all skills which she rightly believed would give her more control of her work in the future.

But music remained important in her life, and she was also using this 'timeout' to perfect her craft. 'I went away. I started to learn how to produce, to understand my own voice. I wanted to be in control. I even taught myself how to edit movies,' she said. 'I was a shy girl, you know. It took me years before I could watch those [Idol] clips.'

If ever she does trawl through the old clips of **Swedish Idol** it will surely stir another memory for her – a romance with fellow contestant and the eventual winner of the series, Daniel Lindstrom. The couple were together for several years, even sharing an apartment in Stockholm for a while before an amicable break up.

But after Daniel, her tv career and a few years away from the business 'hanging around hippie communities' as she describes it, Loreen couldn't ignore the fact that music was in her blood and thoughts of being back on stage were becoming hard to ignore. 'I was just trying to find my way, wherever I went', she said. But eventually she became sure that she wanted to work with music.

She got her chance, in another competitive environment, when she entered Melodifestivalen – the biggest singing competition in Sweden.

Loreen's songs on Swedish Idol

Week one - *If I Ain't Got You* - Alicia Keys

Week two - *Just Like a Pill* - Pink

Week three - *I Wish* - Stevie Wonder

Week four - *Vill Ha Dig* - Freestyle (Featured on the post-competition *Idol* compilation album)

Week five - *Stronger* - Britney Spears

Week six - *(Where Do I Begin) Love Story* - Shirley Bassey

Week seven - *(I've Had) The Time of My Life* - Bill Medley and Jennifer Warnes

Week eight - *Every Breath You Take* - Police

Thriller - Michael Jackson

26 loreen *She's The One*

Loreen performs at the celebrations of Crown Princess Victoria's 35th birthday on July 14, 2012 in Borgholm, Sweden

swedish idol

loreen *She's The One*

melodifestivalen

When Loreen got the chance to compete in Melodifestivalen - Sweden's annual song contest to choose the country's entry for the Eurovision Song Contest - she knew the stakes were high.

Melodifestivalen is a cultural phenomenon in Sweden, generating massive media attention and sparking conversations and debates throughout the nation. It's one of the major events in the nation's cultural and tv calendar and always features among the most popular television shows of the year. In its 60-plus year history it has featured iconic performances, memorable songs, and unforgettable moments that have become a part of Swedish pop culture - including the emergence of Abba back in 1974, before Loreen was born.

As well as launching the careers of many successful artists, Melodifestivalen has also provided a platform for songwriters, composers, and producers - both established and emerging talents. The winning song, along with other popular entries, frequently tops the Swedish charts.

The shows are also visual spectacles, featuring innovative staging concepts and pushing the boundaries of production, lighting, and special effects.

Yet Loreen entered the contest apparently oblivious to its incredible legacy. Unlike almost half the population of Sweden, she hadn't grown up watching Melodifestivalen or Eurovision and it hadn't featured in her life as an adult. 'Honestly, I didn't know anything about Eurovision', she told the *HuffPost* website. 'People don't know, I'm a hippie. I was hanging around these hippie communities, I was somewhere else, working on myself. And so by coincidence this platform came into my life, and obviously, I believe that things come into your life for a reason.'

Melodifestivalen

➤ Sweden's annual Melodifestivalen song contest has been running for over 60 years since the inaugural competition in 1959. Open to established artists and aspiring musicians alike, the competition attracts thousands of song submissions every year, and a jury appointed by the organisers, Sweden's public broadcasters Sveriges Television (SVT) and Sveriges Radio (SR) selects the entries to compete in the live shows, consisting of a series of four semi-finals, a second chance round, and a grand final.

➤ The semi-finals are held in different cities across Sweden and the viewers, along with an expert jury, decide two winners from each round.

➤ The second chance round, known as 'Andra Chansen,' provides an opportunity for acts that did not qualify directly from the semi-finals to compete for a place in the grand final. Four 'duels' are held, where two singers face off against each other. The winner of each duel secures a spot in the final, completing the line-up of 12 finalists.

➤ The grand final of Melodifestivalen attracts millions of viewers in Sweden and abroad. The finalists deliver their performances one last time, and the winner goes on to represent Sweden at the Eurovision Song Contest.

➤ The competition has produced seven winning songs and 26 top-five Eurovision songs for Sweden.

➤ In addition to its entertainment value, Melodifestivalen is a significant economic driver for Sweden, attracting tourists from across Europe to the live shows.

Christer Björkman, the producer of Sweden's Melodifestivalen, had heard Loreen sing when he visited a studio where she was working and was so impressed that he said she 'needs' to be in the competition.

'Everybody was so hyped, like, "oh my god you need to do this", and I was like, "...is it the right way to go? Is this where I'm supposed to go?"' said Loreen.

'I was a little bit confused at first, because I'd been on [Swedish] *Idol* ... and I was a little bit against competing in music... but I just intuitively felt that I needed to do this. I think it was Christer's enthusiasm around my music, and he really believed in my vision'.

Her opportunity to perform in this iconic show in 2011 came thanks to the song *My Heart Is Refusing Me* which she co-wrote with Moh Denebi and Björn Djupström. Like the *Idol* competition, Loreen had to come through one of four heats, with seven songs in each. Those placed first and second went through to the final automatically, while the songs placed third and fourth went into an additional round called Andra Chansen, meaning second chance.

Having been placed fourth in her second semi-final in Gothenburg on 12 February 2011, Loreen went through to the second chance round which was held on 19 February in Linköping.

However she lost her sing off against Sara Varga singing *Run for Life*. For many people that painful, 'almost' moment would have left them dejected. But it was not the end as far as Loreen was concerned.

My Heart Is Refusing Me was released as a single on 11 March 2011 and became one of the biggest hits of the year on the Swedish singles chart, where it spent 19 weeks after debuting and peaking at #9. She was back in business. Resilient as ever she entered Melodifestivalen again the following year – this time with the song *Euphoria,* written by Thomas G:Son and Peter Boström.

Celebrating the songwriters

Euphoria was written by Thomas G:son and Peter Boström.

Thomas G:son

Thomas, whose real surname is Gustafsson, is hugely experienced in writing Eurovision songs, having written a string of entries for national selection contests across Europe, including Scandinavia, Spain, and Cyprus. 13 of his compositions have reached the finals, but Euphoria was his first win.

Peter Boström

Peter Boström is a Swedish music producer also known as Bassflow, who has over 20 Melodifestivalen entries to his name. He had the strange experience of coming first and last at the 2012 Eurovision because as well as co-writing Loreen's winner *Euphoria*, he had also co-written the Norwegian entry *Stay* which languished at the bottom of the leader board with just seven points.

melodifestivalen 33

> *Loreen performs on stage during the Popstars Live Final Show on September 20, 2012 in Berlin, Germany*

Single spotlight – My Heart Is Refusing Me

My Heart Is Refusing Me has gone on to become a real fan favourite. Co-written by Loreen, Björn Djupström and Moh Denebi, the song was Loreen's first entry at Melodifestivalen in 2011 and featured on Loreen's 2012 debut album *Heal*. Its haunting melody perfectly showcases Loreen's vocals. Since Loreen won Eurovision in 2023 it has been picked up by a whole new audience and passed 20 million streams on Spotify.

The song was perfect for Loreen's powerful and emotive vocals which soared over an uplifting, trance EDM (electronic dance music) beat.

Euphoria stormed into the top two, going directly to the final, when Loreen sang it during the first round of Melodifestivalen 2012 on 4 February at the Vida Arena in Vaxjo.

The final was on 10 March at the Globen Arena in Stockholm. While the competition's heats had attracted an average 3.3 million viewers, an estimated 4m watched the final - almost half the country's adult population. Loreen received the highest number of points from both the juries and the public vote, finishing with a grand total of 268 points after a reported 670,000 people voted for her.

She had done it. She was to represent Sweden in Eurovision and at last had the chance to showcase her talent on a global stage......

Hall of Fame

Along with Loreen, Thomas and Peter were elected to the Melodifestivalen Hall of Fame in 2020 for achieving 'Sweden's fifth victory in the Eurovision Song Contest, a groundbreaking number, and a landslide victory, with *Euphoria* (2012).

If that seems a little after the event, it's because SVT, the Swedish national broadcaster, only launched the Melodifestivalen Hall of Fame in 2020 to celebrate the 60th edition of its popular song contest.

There were 48 inaugural inductees, each receiving the *Guldstjärna* (Gold Star) trophy.

Single spotlight – Sober

Loreen's single *Sober,* which had been released as a digital download on 12 September 2011 in Sweden, reappeared in the singles charts, in March 2012 peaking at #26 following her victory at Melodifestivalen with *Euphoria*.

melodifestivalen

Loreen performs at Stockholm Pride 2012 on August 3, 2012 in Stockholm, Sweden

euphoria

Momentum began to build behind Loreen and *Euphoria* as soon as she won Melodifestivalen.

The buzz around her was so intense that by the time of the Eurovision final in Baku, Azerbaijan, on 26 May 2012, most bets were off as bookmakers, fans, and journalists alike had her down as the winner.

So, although Loreen and her team certainly took nothing for granted, it was no surprise in the arena when she won the contest convincingly, providing Sweden with its fifth Eurovision trophy.

Her victory was resounding. She trounced the other entrants by finishing with 372 points, well over 100 more than the second placed act, Buranovskiye Babushki, the popular 'Grannies' from Russia. With its huge hook and synth-layered pulse, Euphoria had proved unforgettable to the national juries and the public alike and she won both votes. Not only that, but Loreen's score was more than the combined points of the bottom 10 acts. 40 out of the 42 voting countries gave her points – with 18 of them awarding *Euphoria* its maximum '12 points'. Bearing in mind that Sweden couldn't vote for itself, this just left Italy as the only country not to include her in its top 10.

It was an incredible result, making Loreen one of the highest scoring winners in the contest's history.

euphoria

loreen *She's The One*

Loreen performs on stage during The Eurovision Song Contest 2012 Grand Final at Crystal Hall on May 26, 2012 in Baku, Azerbaijan

euphoria

Despite topping the leader board, Loreen didn't immediately realise that she had won. 'When I sat there and got all these points, I thought "OK, now it's time for people to vote." I said to Christer Björkman [leader of the Swedish delegation] "Why is everybody cheering?" and he said "What?! You've won, you need to go on stage, man!"'

With a song and performance that was simply outstanding, she had done things 'her way' and changed the competition for the better going forward.

But her success did not come without its struggles. Behind the scenes, the run up to the final show was fraught with difficulties and Loreen needed to draw on all her stores of strength and self-belief as she fought to give the performance she believed the song deserved. Producers of the show became concerned that her staging and appearance didn't sit within the Eurovision 'norms'.

Loreen's favoured dark, simple, and minimal staging, shot through with strobe lighting, was continually questioned, along with her decision to keep her own appearance toned down to help create the mood she wanted and ensure that the vocals dominated. 'Is this going to work?' she remembers being asked by producers in the lead-up to the contest. Nobody thought that 'dark' t would work. She had to battle for the right to perform as she wanted. Even her decision to go barefoot caused palpitations for a director who tried to persuade her to wear some high heels.

Although she stood (without heels) firm, Loreen admitted afterwards that she was a bit nervous about going against all received wisdom. The fact that everybody else was afraid, made her afraid – but she felt strongly that she had to follow her intuition. As a hugely spiritual person she usually acts on her 'gut-feel'.

Then just hours before her first performance, a producer told her that they would need to cut the siren at the start of the song. As Loreen told *Huffpost,* 'I told him, we need the siren at the beginning to neutralise the space. He said, "If you have the siren, you're going to kill the song". Basically I was told, "You're jeopardising the whole thing". This was very late, I was exhausted, it was just before midnight, … so I said, "It's either the siren or I'm out".'

She won the day, but with many of the production team anxious, stressed, and frustrated, she needed nerves of steel to stick to her guns. Her refusal to compromise was partly because she had realised that trying to satisfy other people's ideas and inclinations, as she had done during *Swedish Idol* was painful for her. She needed creative control of her own performance to do herself, and the song, justice.

She was proved right. Her performance during the final on 26 May 2012 was incredible and visually stunning. Many have described it as a piece of pure theatre, movement and song delivered with energy and emotion. Loreen took the demanding interpretive dance moves from noted Stockholm-based choreographer Ambra Succi and executed them flawlessly while never missing a note, despite accidentally swallowing some of the fake snow which falls towards the end of the song.

Explaining more about her performance, Loreen told the *Official Eurovision Song Contest Podcast* that her concept was about female energy and male energy. 'We have a perception of female energy that's about being feminine and being very gentle and sweet. I wanted to show that I, being barefoot and female in this performance, was powerful; something you would call male energy, right? I was playing with the female and the male when Ausben [Ausben Jordan, the male dancer who joined her towards the end of the song] came in - a different entity, being male.

'What I did was to just show that these are two different energies, but they're still very powerful. And they're playing with each other. And it's beautiful. There is no hierarchy. Both energies are needed. And when they are in their own powers, and they're full, they're so healthy for each other.

'This was basically the first performance that I created and the first song where I didn't compromise. I'm gonna go straight with what my intuition is telling me. And so winning that contest with a concept that was purely a reflection of me inside; that was such a statement for myself. It was almost like life told me this is what happens when you trust your intuition.'
Staging aside, Loreen herself looked magnificent, her long hair flowing along with the billowing sleeves of her diaphanous long gold jacket which she wore on top of a simple black jumpsuit.

Some of Sweden's Eurovision winners. (From left) Richard Herrey and Per Herrey, Carola Häggkvist, Måns Zelmerlöw, Loreen and Björn Ulvaeus

Masters of Eurovision

Sweden has won the Eurovision Song Contest seven times: in 1974, 1984, 1991, 1999, 2012, 2015 and 2023, tied with Ireland for the most wins for any country.

The 1974 Eurovision winner **Waterloo** from Abba began Sweden's run of success and has subsequently been voted the most popular Melodifestivalen song of all time and the most popular Eurovision song of the contest's first 50 years.

Apart from its seven outright victories, Sweden consistently achieves strong placements in the Eurovision Song Contest, with its entries frequently landing in the top 10, on the vital 'left hand side' of the leader board. 26 have made the top five. It's a Eurovision powerhouse.

Loreen is crowned the winner of The Eurovision Song Contest 2012 Grand Final at Crystal Hall on May 26, 2012 in Baku, Azerbaijan

But most of all her vocal performance blew most other acts out of the water. She had put her heart and soul into those precious three and a half minutes on stage. There's a sweet moment 30 seconds in when the steely gaze with which she began is replaced by a smile as the audience begin to clap and cheer.

Despite knowing she had done her best, Loreen was stunned as the votes poured in from all corners of Europe. Then, as her achievement sunk in, she had an awakening moment telling her that she was right to follow her gut. 'When I won, I was standing there, waiting to do the

Euphoria

Euphoria was released on 26 February 2012 as the third single from her debut studio album *Heal*. Following the Eurovision Song Contest, it became a runaway hit all over Europe and an international club smash.
Many fans still consider it the gold-standard Eurovision song.

Among its achievements:

➤ Most downloaded Eurovision song ever

➤ Six consecutive weeks at #1 in the Swedish charts

➤ 360,000 units sold in Sweden where it was certified 9xPlatinum

➤ Topping the charts in 16 countries during 2012 and 2013 including Austria, Germany, and Finland

➤ #3 in the UK Singles Chart, the highest position for a non-UK Eurovision entry for 25 years

➤ Sales of 2m copies worldwide

➤ Most successful Eurovision song of the decade

➤ Certified gold, platinum or multiplatinum in over 12 countries

performance again, and there was just something speaking to me in that moment. And what it said was " ...when you follow your intuition, everything flows". I was standing there, and I was overwhelmed. Everything was connected.'

Years after the win she described Euphoria as 'my soul, my spirit. That was the first time in my life where I dared to open up and sing my truth. Before then I was compromising, which is physically painful for me.'

The track itself was highly acclaimed by music critics and fans alike. The high-energy, synthesised Eurodance track was catchy and built to a powerful crescendo, which was easy to sing along with. In fact Loreen has joked since that she never gets to sing this song herself at concerts as the audience always sings with her.

As the head of the Swedish delegation Christer Björkman put it; 'What makes me most happy is that we won with something that I think is good for the Eurovision song contest. It's a very good pop song with a unique artist who did a show that is very modern and daring and very arty. It's not a song you've heard a million times before. This is very special, something new, something unique.' Eurovision fans still consider the song to be a masterpiece.

Thanks to her landslide victory the mononymous 'Loreen' was now known throughout Europe as *Euphoria* stormed the charts at home and abroad. Her 2011 single *My Heart Is Refusing Me* had renewed momentum and re-entered the Swedish charts for 11 weeks.

That same year she picked up the MTV Europe Music Award for Best Swedish Act, two Rockbjörnen Swedish music awards, for Female Artist of the Year and Song of the Year and was also nominated in the World Music Awards.

Loreen was everywhere. But nevertheless her fans were clamouring for more ...in particular they eagerly awaited a full studio album ...it did not disappoint.

loreen *She's The One*

heal

Having now shot to stardom following her Eurovision win, Loreen went on to top the charts with her highly anticipated debut full-length studio album *Heal*, released on 24 October 2012.

Primarily composed of electronica, synth-heavy dance-pop tracks, with dashes of R&B, it was spectacular, complementing *Euphoria* perfectly.

Apple Music described the album as 'Stacked with sweeping singles in the vein of Euphoria (*Crying Out Your Name* and *In My Head*) the singer's big throated heartbreak is in stark relief to the album's electrifying hyper-modern production . In the rare moments her tone is subdued (*Do We Even Matter* and *Heal)*, Loreen's expressive gifts as a vocalist are on display'.

It was a huge commercial success in the charts, a #1 hit in Sweden - where it went on to be certified Platinum for sales above 40,000 units - and charting at #7 in Switzerland, #16 in Germany, and #26 in Austria.

Several tracks were released as singles, *Euphoria* (February 2012) was the lead single, *My Heart Is Refusing Me* was released in international markets in a new remixed version as the second single (October 2012), *Crying Out Your Name* was released in Sweden only as the third single (October 2012) and *In My Head* was the fourth single (February 2013). A fifth track *We Got the Power* was released as the lead single from the reissued version of *Heal* in May 2013.

Loreen performs on stage during The Eurovision Song Contest 2013 Semi-final 1 at Malmö Arena on May 14, 2013 in Malmö, Sweden

Single spotlight – Crying Out Your Name

Single-wise, Loreen's follow up to Euphoria was Crying Out Your Name written by Ana Diaz, Niklas Jarl, Moh Denebi, Gino Yonan, Svante Halldin and Jakob Hazell. Scandipop said that it included all the main elements of a Loreen 'classic …ethereal dance music, a gut wrenching melody, and a big dose of drama laden VOX. We love that this is a great deal longer than most of her previous output though – at three minutes and 38 seconds, there's more of it to enjoy'.

loreen *She's The One*

Sober which had been previously released as a digital download in Sweden (September 2011) was remixed for the album.

Heal received praise for its atmospheric and moody production, with the album's soundscapes often described as cinematic, with rich textures and a sense of grandeur.

Loreen's own songwriting (she collaborated on seven of the album's 12 tracks) was also commended for its storytelling around universal experiences including love, empowerment, and personal growth.

The album's success and critical acclaim, coupled with her new Eurovision fame solidified Loreen's standing as one of Sweden's most talented and respected artists. It also paved the way for her to explore new artistic directions - but the big question around that was would something 'different' be popular with her new fans?

Heal - tracklisting

In My Head

My Heart Is Refusing Me

Everytime

Euphoria

Crying Out Your Name

Do We Even Matter

Sidewalk

Sober

If She's The One

Breaking Robot

See You Again

Heal (ft Blanks)

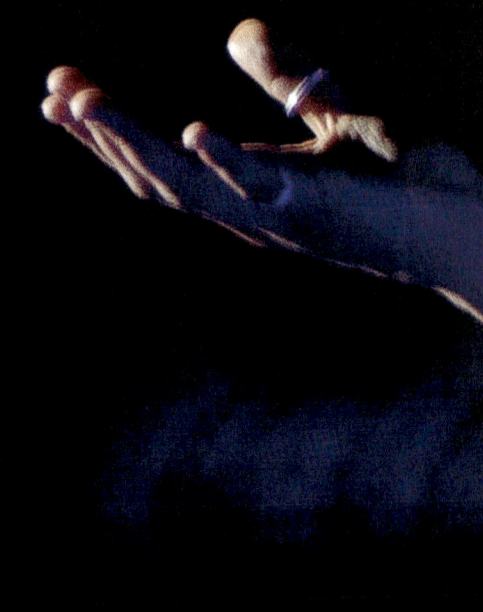

heal | 55

Loreen performs live in 'La noche de Cadena 100' at the Madrid sports palace on March 23, 2013 in Madrid, Spain

loreen *She's The One*

Loreen performs live in 'Art on Ice' at the Globe Arena on March 13, 2014 in Stockholm, Sweden

loreen *She's The One*

Loreen performs at Life Ball 2015 on May 15, 2015 in Vienna, Austria

As reigning Eurovision champion she got the chance to perform at the 2013 European Song Contest held – thanks to her win the year before - in Malmö, Sweden. She used the slot to premiere her new single *We Got the Power* as part of a medley including *My Heart Is Refusing Me* and *Euphoria*. Again her performance was outstanding. She looked spectacular. As it began she was wearing an extravagantly feathered shoulder piece, before changing into a long-trained cloak for the climax of her performance for which she rose into the air. It's hard to forget a Loreen show.

Next came a tour around Finland, Sweden, and Switzerland, including performances as part of the 2014 Art on Ice tour which combined live music with performances from figure skaters.

In January 2014 Loreen got the chance to take part in an exciting collaboration. Swedish STV resurrected its prize-winning series *Sapmi Sessions* which involved well-known Swedish artists travelling north to work with their talented counterparts in the Sámi population. Sámi-speaking people live in Sapmi, which encompasses large northern parts of Scandinavia and the Kola Peninsula in Russia, formerly known as Lapland.

Loreen performs live during a concert at the Postbahnhof on April 11, 2014 in Berlin, Germany

Single spotlight – Under ytan

Under ytan - meaning 'under the surface' in English - was a cover of a 1994 song by Swedish pop singer Uno Svenningsson which Loreen released in December 2015 as her first single in the Swedish language. Originally a guitar pop track, Loreen's version was very different - a moody electro ballad which starts and ends with a sparing mix of voice and synth, building to an instrumental crescendo more than matched by Loreen's powerful vocals to give a rich and dramatic sound.

trying something new

> *The Swedish stars and their Sámi partners were each given three days to write and record a new song together.*

Loreen featured in the first episode, working with Sámi singer Ingá-Máret Gaup-Juuso. Initially Loreen seemed tentative about the project, particularly its tight timescale. 'It's crazy that I'll write a song in three days,' she said on camera. 'It has never happened. I usually sit and work on my songs for three months! But this is a good challenge.'

But she 'clicked' with Ingá-Máret and was inspired by her traditional Sámi 'joik' singing style, which is similar to chanting. The wilderness of their location by Lake Vássejávri, 3600km north of Stockholm, provided a further spiritual and creative boost.

After explaining that her songwriting process generally involved sitting at the piano and simply trying out melodies - 'nothing complicated' as Loreen put it, she and Ingá-Máret worked well together and came up with a song called *Son*. At the time it was mooted as a track on Loreen's next album - but that was a long time coming.

If fans have any criticism of Loreen - which they rarely do - it's that they don't hear enough from her. Rumours that she was 'in the studio' would come and go over the next few years. In 2014 she announced that her second album would be called *Paperlight* and feature collaborations with Canadian singer and multi-instrumentalist Kiesza with whom she'd been working in the studio. She hinted that it would be departure from her most famous song *Euphoria*, describing it as 'dirtier and more hip hop'. She also announced that songs *Jupiter Drive* and *Dumpster* would be singles from the forthcoming album, which was scheduled for release that August.

After a few singles in 2015 - *Paper Light (Higher), Under ytan,* and *I'm in It with You* - things went quiet. Word on the street was that the delay was caused by management and label changes.

trying something new

She had also been very busy with performing. As well as undertaking a short tour, she had completed a residency in Malmö, Sweden, done some private shows and joined in with the Eurovision celebration show put on to mark the contest's 60th anniversary - *Eurovision Song Contest's Greatest Hits* in London in 2015.

In a 2017 interview with YouTube channel *Lady Jenevia*, Loreen reflected on why she hadn't released more material in the five years following *Euphoria* and *Heal*.

'Looking back I think it's because I'm really bad at doing two things at the same time,' she said. 'I really tried for a while, being out there, gigging and playing and doing shows. *Euphoria* was such a huge hit. We thought that after a year or two it would die down a bit and give more space and room for creating new music. And I really tried hard to create music at the same time as playing, but it really didn't work for me because I need to be so focussed on one thing. I give everything I have, so if it's a show then I am all into that, like focussing on how is this going to look, how is the scenery, blah blah blah and all the details. I think looking back that is one of the main reasons. I created music and then I was out playing and then coming back I'd try to finish it up, but I couldn't because I'd developed, and I wanted to create new music.'

But then in 2016 she finally found some time. She said she had been writing 'lots'. Her work included a song for which she had high hopes. It was called *Statements* and became her entry for Melodifestivalen 2017. The Eurovision Queen was risking her royal status by returning to the qualifying competition…

Single spotlight - Paper Light (Higher)

Pape Light (Higher) was originally announced as the lead single from the planned *Paper Light* album and released in March 2015. Loreen performed it at that year's Melodifestivalen where she was the interval act. Upbeat and peppy, it showed Loreen was experimenting with a new musical direction while retaining her electronic and dance influences. The new sound went down well, and the song reached #2 on the Swedish singles chart. The album however didn't ever appear.

trying something new

65

Loreen photographed on October 16, 2012 in Stockholm, Sweden

making a statement

Loreen frequently speaks about needing to have something to say in her songs. It's the main reason she creates. 'I totally respect people who write about things which are more trivial because you need that too, but for me I have to have something with more substance, that's bigger than myself,' she explains.

She certainly felt that way about her 2016 song **Statements**, a commentary on modern-day Swedish politics, which she co-wrote with a new production team called The Family, comprising Joy Deb, Linnea Deb and Anton Hård af Segerstad.

Her words and performance were full of conviction, inciting people to 'do something' as the shouted refrain 'statements' is followed by the line 'we don't need no ...statements'. Literally action speaks louder than words. 'It's about the situation in the world today,' said Loreen. 'But above all, it's about giving people power and inspiration. That's what we need today.'

She believed in the song so much that she took the brave decision to enter it into Melodifestivalen 2017. It was not an easy decision and she said that she only finally decided the day before the press conference which would announce the contestants. 'I thought so many different things,' she said. 'Should I or should I not? Why? And then I realised that I have something to say and would like to convey to everyone.

'I know many people do not know why I came back after *Euphoria*. Are you trying to beat Euphoria? No. It had its own chapter five years ago. This time I need something else.'

She went on to take part in the fourth semi-final on 25 February 2017 in Skellefteå, where in true Loreen style she put her heart and soul into a moody and mysterious performance. Although she failed to qualify directly to the final, her third place finish meant she went through to compete in the Andra Chansen/Second Chance round. This time she was in a duel competing against an 18-year-old up and coming YouTube star, singer and guitarist Anton Hagman.

making a statement   67

Speculating on her chances at Andra Chansen, Loreen said that with her performance being so unlike the usual Eurovision fare, and with the song also being very different, she was just hoping to get another chance to sing it. 'I'm not doing this to win. I've already done that. I'm doing this for another reason.'

However, the song was strong, and The Family had a great track record too which included having written *Heroes* for Swedish star Måns Zelmerlöw which won Melodifestivalen and went on to win Eurovision in 2015.

Anton's song, *Kiss You Goodbye*, was simple but melodic and he performed it with charm – and as one commentator put it, 'puppy dog eyes'. Even Loreen described him as 'drop dead gorgeous' so he certainly caught viewers' attention. His simple staging, just him and his guitar, was completely different from Loreen's dark and dramatic rendition of *Statements.* Her energetic staging included four additional dancers working alongside her to conjure imagery around historical moments featuring powerful women, referencing the French Revolution and 'The Woman with the Handbag' - a photograph famous in Sweden for capturing the moment a woman hit a marching Neo-Nazi with her handbag.

Possibly some of this was lost on the audience who instead fell for the good looks of young Anton, preferring his more traditional pop song and delivery over Loreen's more challenging piece.

As one tweet that night put it, 'politics and music don't go together'. And it seemed the Saturday night tv audience of voters agreed as Anton won the sing off and went through to the final (where he eventually finished 10th) and Loreen was out.

While her fans were stunned, Loreen herself appeared sanguine, reflecting afterwards that perhaps it was down to her 'very frustrated, angry energy' coming across in the performance. She did admit that her ego took a hit but thought that it did no harm for a person to be brought back to earth sometimes. Her mature reaction showed how much she had grown as a person and an artist since competing in her first Melodifestivalen when she told music website Scandipop that she hadn't read any of the press coverage around the competition because 'I get so affected by it. I am a sensitive person...yeah I'm extremely sensitive.'

It isn't too unusual for previous winners to reappear at Melodifestivalen, but taking part again comes with a heavy weight of pressure and expectation. And mostly those artists get through to the final at the very least. It was a sobering experience for Loreen and her team and it must have stung a little.

But she didn't dwell on the matter for too long. She said that overall the response to her 'special and specific story' had been positive, and she was glad that people cared and wanted things to be better. 'That was the whole point [of **Statements**] ' she said. 'I hope people are inspired by the fact that I'm standing up for something and dared to do that.

Alongside her efforts around **Statements,** Loreen had been working on her much anticipated new music. After six years with Warner, she was now signed to BMG Scandinavia, and she promised in several interviews that there would be an EP in the spring and a full album in the fall. After her previous false starts around album release promises, this time she said, with a laugh, that if anything got in the way to stop the release ... 'kill me'.

She promised that the forthcoming EP and album would represent a new 'chapter' and be a departure from her previous work, describing it as 'raw, vintage, organic and with a little twist of hip hop'.

In the meantime, fans got a hint of what was to come, along with some in-depth interviews and behind the scenes footage of Loreen's life, in September when Swedish public broadcaster SVT released an in-depth documentary on the singer in 2017.

Called **Livet enligt Loreen** (Life According to Loreen) the film had been several years in the making as SVT reporter Bengt Norborg joined Loreen on a visit to her mother Choumicha in Västeras, and to the extended family home in Morocco, as well as watching her at work in the studio.

making a statement

Loreen was in a reflective and open mood as she stressed once again that she was not attempting to recreate *Euphoria* when she wrote new music. Challenged over whether her failure to match its success in the intervening years made her a 'one hit wonder' Loreen was thoughtful as she explained, 'I do not know, do not think so much about it... A creative process obviously takes time. But through these years I have had creative dips. The reason has been that when you create and do not get creative outlets, - then you will end up - at least I do - in a creative dipping'.

Loreen also spoke about her own creativity and integrity and how she had to work hard to protect both. 'Things change all the time. I change. The most difficult thing is that many people are very disappointed that some of what it used to be is not the same. I am always me. I may have a little 'hard' side because I've had to be a bit tougher to stand for me.' She also referenced how she would agonise over making decisions because she had a fear of failure. For the same reason she needs an input into all her work. 'I don't like swimming in deep water because I have no control'.

In the documentary Loreen played some of the new album, the tracks *71 Charger* and *Love Me America*, which compared to her old music she said was 'more honest and scaled down... A little more naked.'

Viewers also saw Loreen's versatility as she sang opera for pleasure as she pottered around - Puccini's soprano aria *O Mio Babbino Caro* - and, this time in a studio - a cover of Jefferson Airplane's *White Rabbit.*

As well as giving an interesting glimpse into Loreen's backstory, this stripped-back portrait whet the appetite for more music. Fans could hardly wait.

making a statement | 73

more music at last

In the event, Loreen's fans had a slightly longer wait than promised as 'spring and fall' became summer and winter.

But in August 2017 came the Nude EP, which included two tracks released as singles, *Body* and *Jungle*. Acknowledging that her fans had stuck around during what had been a fairly fallow period, music release-wise, Loreen took to Instagram to announce ' The wait is over. Today I released **'Body'** - part one of my #Nude project, a project just for you all'.

Body, proved to be a trance track layering some quite breathy vocals over a club beat, while

Nude - tracklisting

Body

Jungle

Ocean Away

Jungle, featuring fellow female Swedish singing star Elliphant, had a slow reggae vibe. The comeback trail seemed like it was going to be varied.

It seems fair to assume that Loreen had at last got the creative freedom she craved.

Then *Ride*, her second studio album, was released on 24 November 2017. More experimental and alternative than her earlier music, *Ride* was predominantly an indie rock-style piece, strongly featuring bass guitar with elements of trip-hop and electronica.

The album peaked at #31 on the Swedish chart. Two singles were released from the album: *71 Charger* (released 29 September 2017) and *Hate the Way I Love You*, (released 27 October 2017). The album had gone through many stages as it included music recorded during the past three years. In a move away from the dance tracks which filled *Heal,* many of the *Ride* tracks were mid-tempo or balladic. Critics noted *Hate the Way I Love You* as a standout track.

Noting the contrast between her Eurovision winner and this new, more experimental work, music website Scandipop said; '2017 is a good year if you're a fan of Loreen (though not necessarily if you're more a fan of *Euphoria*)' and went on to describe *Hate the Way I Love You* as; 'A song that starts off as a stark and atmospheric ballad, before morphing into a Björk-esque dose of pulsating euphoria. Ok, maybe euphoria is an inappropriate word to use in the same sentence as Loreen these days.'

With three songs on *Nude* and a further 10 on *Ride*, Loreen released more tracks in 2017 than she had done in total in the five years between 2012's *Heal* and 2017's *Statements*.

Yet none of the new music really made the impact of either of those pieces of work. And she still hadn't had a hit to match *Euphoria* since 2012.

Loreen spoke about this in an interview, saying; 'People compare everything you do, even subconsciously. Every time you come out with something that is a little bit darker and something completely different, they have a hard time accepting it.'

Ride – tracklisting
(Loreen was credited as a co-writer on all of them)

71 Charger

Dreams

Jupiter Drive

Fire Blue

Hate the Way I Love You

I Go Ego

Heart on Hold

Love Me America

Ride

71 Charger (Strings bonus track)

But she was unwavering in her determination to do things her way. This included featuring in a couple of more 'fun' projects which surprised and delighted fans.

The first was a cameo in the 2020 Netflix musical comedy, *Eurovision Song Contest: The Story of Fire Saga,* starring Will Ferrell. Loreen appears in the famous 'party' scene where she, and other iconic Eurovision contestants including fellow winners Austria's Conchita Wurst, Israel's Netta, and Norway's Alexander Rybak, cover a mash up of tracks. Loreen sang part of the Cher song *Believe* before segueing seamlessly into *Ray of Light* by Madonna.

Her next project also involved reinterpreting music as she took part in the hit Swedish show *Så Mycket Bättre* (So Much Better) in which famous artists cover classic songs. Loreen performed an acclaimed rendition of *Jag är en vampyr* (I am a vampire) which had been a huge hit in Sweden in 2008 for Scandinavian singer/songwriter Markus Krunegård.

Then came her first-ever acting role. Loreen was asked to play Maria, the young Moroccan mother of the main character John-John, in the 2021 Netflix romantic drama movie JJ+E . It was a remake of the 1996 Swedish drama film Vinterviken about two star-crossed young lovers, John-John (JJ) and Elisabeth.

JJ and Elisabeth both live in Stockholm, but they are miles apart financially and culturally. JJ comes from a rough housing estate where he lives in a tenement with his immigrant single mother (played by Loreen) and her boyfriend, while Elisabeth is from a prosperous suburb and lives in a more prosperous part of town in a swanky house with a pool.

Discussing the movie, Loreen said that she took the part of JJ's mother knowing she would be able to draw on the experiences of her own mother Choumicha, as well as those of her grandmother and great-grandmother. The film was notable for its depiction of Sweden's multicultural underclass.

Whether it's music or movies, the hardships of womanhood are a constant source of inspiration for Loreen. She said it was the aspect of the film that most encouraged her to take on this powerful part.

But it was back to business with more music when Loreen released her first self-written Swedish single, called ***Sötvattentårar (Freshwater Tears)*** in March 2021. In an interview with SVT to discuss her foray into Swedish language singing, Loreen said that while she had felt the need to sing in Swedish for some time she had never had the time because she was singing in English to satisfy and communicate with a worldwide fan base.

But things changed during the Covid 19 pandemic, when like many other artists, Loreen was forced to take some time out and had some time to experiment.

Having sung other people's songs in Swedish she knew how it sounded, but hadn't quite appreciated the full force of putting across an emotion in your first language. 'It was like getting to know yourself', she said. 'When you sing in English and it's not even a native language, there is a small distance between what you are saying… to say 'I love you' … I can throw myself into that, but to say 'Jag alskar dig' (the phrase in Swedish) has an impact which I was not aware of before'.

more music at last

loreen *She's The One*

more music at last | 81

Loreen performing during The Great Eurovision Song Contest concert 2022 in the Ziggo Dome November 17, 2022 in Amsterdam, Netherlands

raising the roof

Post-pandemic, life was getting back to normal for everyone and Loreen issued a new single, *Neon Lights*, as part of a campaign partnership with Lexus NX cars in May 2022. She was excited to reboot her recording career under a new label, having signed with Universal Music Group in 2020. She described the song as very spiritual, but with a 'Kill Bill' vibe.

She had co-written it with Maria Smith - one half of the Swedish pop-folk duo Smith & Thell - and Swedish rapper Petter "Professor P" Tarland. It was an electropop track heavily featuring synthesisers, but also incorporating some elements of her Moroccan heritage.

"I'm extremely nerdy when it comes to synths, especially analogue synths. So much so that these days I build my entire live shows around them. I felt that I wanted to bring that sound into the studio and simply act like I was in a *Terminator* movie. That's how *Neon Lights* came about. It's an initial introduction to the new soundscape that I'm creating,' she explained in an interview with pop music blog Muumuse.

It was around this time that Loreen also referenced channelling an alpha-female 'character' to allow her to access different parts of her personality, saying, 'I like the feeling of creating characters in my songs who reflect both the parts of me that I have and parts that I wish existed. In my upcoming music, I focus on an alpha female of sorts, a contemporary Joan of Arc, who is to try to save the world. I explore different parts of her in different songs.'

From *Euphoria*, through *Paperlights* to *Neon Lights*, Loreen was now an established artist with an impressive, if slightly thin, back catalogue. No-one really expected to see her singing competitively again –least of all Loreen herself.

That was until an embryonic song called *Tattoo* arrived in her inbox. This dramatic dance-pop anthem explores a troubled romantic relationship using the tattoo as a metaphor for the fact that, despite the difficulties and obstacles the couple may face, Loreen's lover has changed her forever and is indelibly ingrained in her soul.

'I remember very clearly it was about 10 in the evening. G:son and the gang sent me the song. I just felt something before I heard the song, I pressed play and it was a very special feeling, almost like falling in love,' Loreen told *The EuroTrip podcast.*

The song was utterly captivating, another anthemic dance-pop track. After a trance-like opening it builds up to a crescendo. Loreen describes its mood as 'a bit mysterious and powerful at the same time'.

Once heard it can't be forgotten- unsurprising given that it was written by a top-notch group of composers. As well as the veteran team of Thomas G:Son and Peter Boström, writers of *Euphoria*, there was input from new talents including Jimmy Jansson, who had broken the record for most entries in one season at Melodifestivalen 2020, Jimmy 'Joker' Thörnfeldt, who has worked with stars including Jennifer Lopez and One Direction and has a proven track record in writing song competition entries, and Cazzi Opeia, who slayed at Melodifestivalen 2022 as the writer and singer of *I Can't Get Enough.* She also co-composed *Wonderland* which was the winning entry for the Eurovision-inspired American Song Contest.

On top of this stellar songwriting line up, Loreen added her input to their demo in the studio. Needing to make the track 'her own' she added a few 'Loreen' touches, so that she also earned a writing credit on the final version. As she explained it, 'If you take someone else's song it must go through your filter and become you.'

But that's jumping ahead ... back in early 2022 Loreen's first reaction to mention of taking *Tattoo* to Eurovision, via Melodifestivalen, was a flat 'NO'.

Despite the powerful song sounding like a perfect mesh between *Euphoria* and Loreen's newer style, she couldn't commit immediately. 'I usually do that when I don't know the purpose of why I'm doing something' she said in an interview with *Rolling Stone*. 'Initially, I said no, because I needed time to figure things out. When I say time to figure things out, what I mean is, I need to understand why I do things."

After weeks of hearing no, she couldn't do it, Loreen's team finally accepted her decision and were about to confirm her non-participation with Melodifestivalen organisers when Loreen suddenly changed her mind. 'I think I confused my whole team,' she laughed during an interview with the Culture Fix channel.

In touch with her feelings as usual, she explained that after first ruling herself out, she felt the energies around the project change. She started to notice 'beautiful' signs that told her that taking *Tattoo* to Melodifestivalen was something she was meant to do. She added that she always likes to take her time when making a decision.

So it was that in November 2022 it was announced that Loreen would enter Melodifestivalen for the fourth time. In the years since her last appearance the contest had remained as colossal as ever. For Swedes it is almost bigger than Eurovision itself, certainly in its scale and length. As ever it toured the country, becoming the talk of the town in each of the hosting cities.

Loreen was scheduled to take part in the last of the semi-finals, which was held in Malmö on 25 February 2023. The anticipation was incredible, and she was the clear favourite, with betting companies saying there was a 91 per cent chance that she would win. All additional pressure when the prize was considered hers to lose.

She was put into the competition's last semi-final, as the last artist to perform. But she didn't mind where or when she sang – what she did care about was that the performance was 'perfect' according to her vision.

loreen *She's The One*

Loreen photographed on April 25, 2023 in Stockholm, Sweden

raising the roof

As she explained, 'The performance is so important...I work really hard to create one hell of a show.

'It starts with the song. But then the thing that happens when I hear music is I see things in pictures. The moment I heard '*Tattoo*' I saw the scene, the scenery, the vibe, the colour, the narrative, and from there I started to build. If I don't see a picture with a song, the song is not for me. It's not a match, you know. I give the visual part a lot of energy because I feel it enhances the music - gives it a face.'

Her stage shows are always unmissable and this one was no exception - in fact it outdid all the others...

The first striking image came when the staging was revealed. Loreen had worked with light, stage and conceptual designer Tobias Rylander to create something really special. The set featured two 4×4 metre LED screens, one of them functioning as a platform, while the other hung from the ceiling directly above it, like a roof. At the start of the performance the screens are close together, with Loreen laying in the middle between them, where the gap is just a couple of feet. Melodifestivalen presenter Jesper Rönndahl likened the effect to two 'hamburger buns' with Loreen sandwiched between them as the 'filling'. Other commentators have described the set up as looking like a 'panini press'. Loreen preferred to liken the setting to her being in a 'mystical small room' as she sang about holding on to the right love that's arrived at the wrong time. Either way it was instantly iconic.

Loreen starts the song laying in the small illuminated enclosed space between the screens and as the song builds, the screens move further apart so that Loreen is eventually able to stand, revealing that the floor of the bottom screen is covered in sand. The top screen becomes a backdrop of incredible LED effects which included mist, a desert storm, and a sunrise to illustrate *Tattoo's* theme of reconnecting with nature. Even Loreen's ultra-long fake fingernails were natural in that they were made of stone. These eye-catching nails, which gave a claw-like element to her hands, were designed to enhance her choreography which involved a lot of hand movements.

The performance began as it should but was then interrupted by an environmental activist who invaded the stage waving a flag, forcing organisers to cut Loreen's song short. It must have been frightening, but a seemingly unruffled Loreen returned to the stage a few minutes later to restart her performance. As if that hadn't been challenge enough, Loreen also faced the potential hazards of slipping on the sandy floor and dealing with the heavy screen right above her head.

But in the event the second performance went without a hitch. Loreen won her semi-final in Malmö outright, progressing straight to the grand final on 11 March. No need for a 'second chance' sing off this time. *Tattoo* was released on digital platforms that same evening, making its Swedish chart debut at #1, giving her a second Swedish #1 single.

By the time of the Grand Final the buzz around Loreen was huge. But she had competition. Having lost out to a smart young man at Melodifestivalen before (we're looking at you Anton Hagman) Loreen must have eyed up fellow contestants 20-year-old dance/pop twins Marcus and Martinus with particular trepidation. Fresh from a win on the Swedish version of *The Masked Singer*, they were on a roll and their song *Air* was a strong contender for Melodifestivalen, along with rock band Smash Into Pieces and their track *Six Feet Under* which had come second to Loreen in the semi-finals.

Whereas the heats are 100 per cent public votes, for the final, there are also votes from national juries. As with the main Eurovision competition, their points 1-7 are put straight on the board while a spokesperson announces the top three songs which are awarded 8, 10 and 12 points respectively. On this occasion the juries came from Croatia, Austria, Latvia, Belgium, Malta, Australia, Germany, and Spain.

The judging began with those jury votes. Possibly to build some dramatic tension, Croatia gave

loreen *She's The One*

raising the roof

91

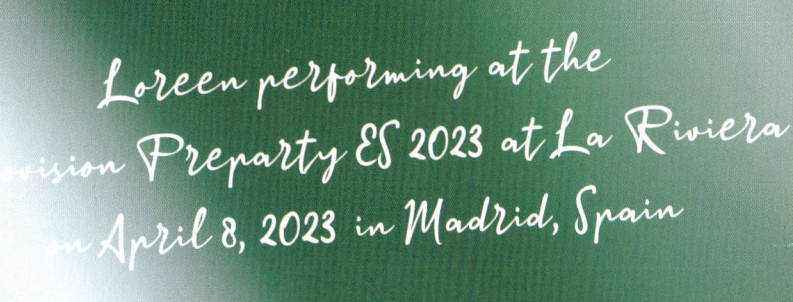

Loreen performing at the
Eurovision Preparty ES 2023 at La Riviera
on April 8, 2023 in Madrid, Spain

their points first, awarding Loreen their 'third' place mark of eight points. But from then on Loreen and *Tattoo* received an avalanche of 12 points from every other jury. This was proving to be more of a coronation than a contest.

But the public votes were still to come and had the potential to change everything. These scores were announced in reverse order so that Loreen, at the top of the leader board, had to wait until last to hear her fate. It was good news – she won with 177 points by a clear margin of 39 points over the second placed act Marcus and Martinus. For once Loreen's usual cool seemed to desert her. She had looked tense during the voting and by the end she was quite emotional as she celebrated her victory.

She was on her way to the main Eurovision competition with the chance to make history as the first woman to win it twice. As she said, 'If the Swedish people want me to represent them in Eurovision it's a commitment, not something you just take on board. Then I will go in there with strength, love and joy'.

Loreen performing at the London Eurovision Party 2023 at Outernet London on April 16, 2023 in London, England

loreen *She's The One*

tattoo

With six Eurovision Song Contest wins and 26 top five places to its name by the start of the 2023 competition, Sweden had left no one in any doubt of its ability to create winning packages.

For the 67th contest in Liverpool the word was that they had done it again. Loreen and *Tattoo* was a brilliant combination of an electrifying, anthemic song, a knockout performance, stunning vocals, and world-class production. Could this be her second and historic Eurovision triumph?

But with commentators declaring that the trophy was Loreen's to lose, the pressure on her was intense. It was also noted as a strongly competitive year. Israel's entry was highly regarded. Sweden's Scandinavian neighbours Finland and Norway had made it to the competition's semi-finals with stupendous and catchy tracks. The other front runner was handsome Marco Mengoni, representing Italy who had generated the second-highest number of Spotify streams with his track *Due Vite* in the month leading up to the finals.

But Loreen could take comfort from the fact that *Tattoo* was the track which had stopped Marco from topping the Spotify chart, attracting twice as many streams as him between 25 March and 25 April 2023.

She was a fan favourite for sure. All the indications were that she would triumph again.

Loreen 2023

Loreen performs at Melodifestivalen 2023

Ukraine had won the 2022 contest, with the Kalush Orchestra and their song *Stefania*, and should have hosted in 2023. But with security concerns following the Russian invasion and subsequent war making this impossible, the event was moved to the UK which had come second with Sam Ryder and *Space Man.* Of the 20 UK cities who expressed an interest in hosting, seven were shortlisted. The city of Liverpool in the northwest won the opportunity, in no small part due to its incredible musical heritage, including, of course, The Beatles.

Loreen thrived in Liverpool where the atmosphere was incredible and full of positive energy. 'The whole city is on fire and the audience is amazing', she said, noting that everything was very different to her previous experience in Baku which she had described as 'tense' following the human rights issues she had confronted there.

So it was a visibly more relaxed Loreen who appeared in a succession of pre-contest publicity events. She looked amazing and was also incredibly well-prepared.

Immediately after her victory at Melodifestivalen, concerns had been raised about how Tattoo's extravagant staging would be transferred to the Liverpool Arena venue. For one thing the 1.8 tonne upper LED screen was too heavy to hang from the rigging as it had done in Sweden. The other consideration was the length of time needed for the set up. While this had been accommodated in the Swedish competition, the Eurovision contest traditionally limited the changeover between acts to just 45 seconds. Plus of course the main Eurovision show includes 37 acts, plus the interval artists, whereas Melodifestivalen only has to accommodate 12 performances.

In the event, despite the challenges that the *Tattoo* staging presented, the Eurovision organisers in Liverpool were able to accommodate a simplified version of the technology, using smaller screens and increased use of lighting for the effect previously given by the top screen to create the required, other-worldly, visual universe.

Loreen performs on stage during The Eurovision Song Contest 2023 Grand Final at M&S Bank Arena on May 13, 2023 in Liverpool, England

One thing unchanged from Melodifestivalen was Loreen's striking costume. It was a figure-hugging, futuristic, faux-leather two piece - a sandy-coloured long-sleeved 'bralette' top and trousers with 'biker knees' and cut out sections and macrame.

Speaking on her TikTok channel, Loreen told fans it had been a tall order to get an outfit that could cope with her performance setting and choreography.

'Life just sent me this amazing designer, Fadi El Khoury and I called him and I said Fadi, I'm sorry. I need an outfit and we have four days. Having an outfit that you can move with... it's really hard core - it's not that easy.'

After rushing over to his studio to brief him on her staging and dance moves, Loreen was delighted that Fadi 'got it'. 'The first sketch was just amazing. I was like, that's it, here it is. When you are in the right space with the right people things just flow.

Fadi El Khoury

Fadi El Khoury is a Swedish/Lebanese couture designer who has dressed everyone from the Swedish royal family to high society Scandinavians and businesswomen around the world. After attending the Ecole Superieure de Mode et des Beaux Arts in Paris, he trained under John Galliano at Christian Dior, and Alber Elbaz at Lanvin.

Fadi El Khoury

loreen *She's The One*

"I was very disciplined & had a strict routine..."

Critical acclaim for Tattoo

Daily Telegraph '...a series of climaxes each more vivid than the next, an intense electro ballad that built to an absolute banger from intimate intro to a dramatic monster with a cute "hoo-hoo-hoo" hook and a sky high chorus. It is genuinely a great, modern, emotional pop song, and you can't say that about every Eurovision winner'.

Neonmusic.co.uk 'The chorus is especially powerful, as Loreen belts out her feelings with conviction and passion. The metaphor of a tattoo is effective in describing how hard it is to erase someone from your memory and your heart. The song also features some beautiful harmonies and vocal layers that add to the richness and complexity of the sound'.

Rolling Stone 'Tattoo is an undeniable banger'.

As well as looking the part, Loreen had prepared herself for her demanding performance physically as well. For months before the shows she had lived in a 'bubble' which she described as being akin to method acting. 'I was very disciplined and had a strict routine for sleep, food, exercise, all those things, to make the song as strong as possible,' she said. 'It is very physically challenging. I had to think, am I strong enough for this. It affects the vocals 100 per cent.'

She had worked with weights and did cardio exercises which she described as 'brutal', to ensure she was as fit as possible and able to control her breathing during the performance so that her vocals didn't suffer as she moved around.

'The rush of adrenaline from a performance makes your pulse go up, so the better your [physical] condition, the calmer you will be,' she explained.

Speaking to TV4's Nyhetsmorgon (News Morning programme) she said that her performance '...had to be pure and real and I had to be in that space, almost like a meditative space ...because that's what the performance stands for.'

So when she took to the stage of the Liverpool Arena for her first semi-final on 9 May, everything was perfect. As when she sang *Euphoria*, she was barefoot again, with her signature long hair flowing and her hands decorated with subtle henna markings, set off by her statement stone manicure.

Despite the fact she remained the runaway favourite, she was taking part in a very strong semi-final show, featuring several of the acts making up her most fierce competition including Israel, Norway, and Finland.

As the points came in it was soon obvious that Loreen would make it through to the grand final. Of the 15 acts who performed that night, five went home, while Loreen progressed comfortably, coming second with 135 points. She was however beaten to the number one spot on the leader board by **Käärijä** from Finland who won 177 points with his very popular, high energy number *Cha Cha Cha*. Did this bode ill for the final?

There wasn't long to wait. The Eurovision grand final was held on 13 May in front of a full-capacity 11,000-strong live audience and more than 160 million people around the world watching on tv.

There were 26 acts in all, 20 through from the semi-final competitions, with the remaining six being last year's winner Ukraine which qualified automatically, along with the 'big five' - UK, France, Germany, Italy and Spain who get automatic entry as the biggest financial contributors towards the event.

Loreen performed 9th out of the final 26 contestants. Her performance was flawless – her vocals, movement and storytelling were all on point. The song was an earworm. She could do no more.

The scoring process began around 10.30pm after the final act had performed. Despite the atmosphere being very intense, Loreen remained unexpectedly calm, explaining that she often ends up in a meditative mode when there is chaos all around.

Storming the set design

Award-winning conceptual and lighting designer Tobias Rylander has made his name by pushing the boundaries of innovative and creative modern design across music tours, fashion, theatre, and commercials.

Most recently he worked on The 1975's critically acclaimed 'At Their Very Best' 2022 world tour, and has also worked on shows for The XX, FKA Twigs, Drake, London Grammar, Robyn, and The Strokes.

Speaking to *Scandinavian Vogue* about his set design for *Tattoo*, Tobias described his artistic connection with Loreen as 'an instant match'. He said she was someone he had always admired for her creativity and integrity, both as an artist and a person. 'We both have very strong gut feelings and it felt like we understood and trusted each other from the start,' he said. 'She had a vision, direction, and aesthetic in mind, which always makes my work easier. It felt very clear and direct and almost like a creative romance.'

He said the incorporation of sand, mist and smoke, wind, sky - even the stone fingernails - were all inspired by nature and by Loreen's Moroccan heritage and nomadic character.

'We knew from the start that we wanted to create a room or a world of her own on stage, to take people's minds off the bling and eye candy that is a Eurovision stage. We knew that we wanted a horizon and an eternal void … A desert and a sandstorm started to feel very natural around Loreen,' he said. 'A storm of sand and smoke that could tell the story of her history, background, and journey. I like to say that Loreen is still a Nomad even if it, in her case, is culturally and musically.'

On top of all that creativity and power, the staging was an incredible engineering feat. Even though the original Melodifestivalen set had to be downsized and adapted for the final in Liverpool, Tobias was unconcerned. 'We all knew Loreen could have sung in the dark and still won that competition,' he said.

Loreen performs at Melodifestivalen 2023

'Nerves were strong especially in my team,' said Loreen. 'So I was in a pretty meditative state of mind because I felt like I needed to balance it out.' The first stage of voting sees points coming in from national juries made up of music professionals from each country. Then the public votes are added to those results.

At the halfway point Loreen had a commanding lead, topping the list with 340 points from the juries, ahead of second placed Israel with 177, Italy on 176, Finland on 150 and Estonia on 146.

The points from the audience votes were then added in reverse order, meaning that Loreen, first in the ranking according to the juries, would be last to have her score amended. It was a tortuous wait, during which time she displayed an almost zen-like calm despite occasional expressions of agony. She would take some beating, but it was possible.

In a fiendishly complex system of weighted scores, the public votes from Europe and the rest of the world, could change everything.

Loreen had entered an exclusive club with just two members – she and Johnny Logan from Ireland are the only people ever to have won Eurovision twice. Johnny won in 1980 and 1987. Strangely both artists were 17th on the running order on the night of their first wins.

In the end the result went to the wire. Finland won 376 points from the public, which saw them fly to the top of the score board with 526 points. The other top placed countries by jury vote, Italy and Israel, did well but didn't get enough public votes to challenge, so that with just the votes for Sweden to come Loreen was the only person standing between Finland and the trophy. But she needed a minimum of 187 points to topple her Scandinavian rival.

During an agonising wait, Loreen could be seen to crack just once as she whispered 'come on' while presenter Graham Norton left the obligatory dramatic pause. Then came the news she needed – 245 points, giving her a winning score of 583. She had done it and entered the history books as only the second artist, and first woman, ever to win Eurovision twice. After accepting the coveted Eurovision trophy of a crystal glass microphone, Loreen described her win as 'overwhelming', adding that she was 'so happy. I'm so thankful. Thank you for this. This is for you. Thank you.'

Loreen claims her second Eurovision title

As well as making Eurovision history, Loreen and her super-strong song also made Spotify history generating more than 60 million streams globally within days and cracking the Spotify Global Top 50. By 14 May, she also held the record for the most-streamed track in a day globally by a female Swedish artist. Sales and streams continue to soar. Even in the US, a Eurovision wasteland, *Tattoo* made its debut on the Billboard Global 200 at #15 and rose to #7 on the Billboard Global Excl.US survey.

Speaking about her win at a post-contest press conference, Loreen said; 'I feel proud. The song has certain values. It's about hope, it's about self-love, it's about strength. It resonates with people. Everything feels surreal. I am seriously overwhelmed. This is so beautiful. One feeling I have in my body that's taken over is just gratitude.'

Having re-claimed her crown, Loreen looks unlikely to be challenged as *Queen of Eurovision* anytime soon. She celebrated by visiting several of her various 'kingdoms' in a short tour during the second half of 2023.

Creative choreography

Loreen's choreography is simple, but with intense emotional expression. Her fluid movements perfectly complement her music and lyrics, while her commanding presence establishes an instant emotional connection with her audience.

One of the most iconic elements of her movement is her use of her hands, as she uses gestures and intricate finger choreography to emphasise the emotions conveyed in her songs. She intersperses her dance moves with moments of stillness, which build tension and physically represent the rising intensity of the music as she appears to live each song.

loreen *She's The One*

The Tattoo tour - 2023

JUNE
4 - The Mighty Hoopla, London, UK

JULY
28- Villa Belparc, Göteborg, Sweden

NOVEMBER
7 - Opium Rooms, Dublin, Ireland
8 - St. Luke's & The Winged Ox, Glasgow, UK
10 - Electric Brixton, London, UK
12 - Paradiso, Amsterdam, Netherlands
14 - Trix, Antwerp, Belgium
15- Metropol, Berlin, Germany
16 - Klub Stodola, Warsaw, Poland
17 - Docks, Hamburg, Germany
19 - Rockefeller Music Hall, Oslo, Norway
20 - Vega, Copenhagen, Denmark
23 - Cirkus Arena, Stockholm, Sweden
26 - Vanha Ylioppilastalo, Helsinki, Finland
27 - Pakkahuone, Tampere, Finland
29 - Noblessner Foundry, Tallinn, Estonia
30 - Palladium, Riga, Latvia

DECEMBER
1 - Kauno Arena, Kaunas, Lithuania
4 - X-TRA, Zurich, Switzerland
5 - Alhambra, Paris, France

Loreen performs at the Mighty Hoopla Festival 2023 at Brockwell Park on June 4, 2023 in London, England

we got the power

A strong sense of purpose runs through Loreen's life. Having been clear since childhood that if she were ever to become famous she would use her platform for good, she has been true to her word.

She believes that she has a responsibility to use her fame, saying that she needs '...to make whatever change I can. There's something bigger than creativity and that's a human life.'

Setting to work as soon as she got the chance, she wasted no time in highlighting the questionable human rights record of Azerbaijan when she was in the country as Sweden's representative in the 2012 Eurovision Song Contest.

Telling reporters that 'human rights are violated in Azerbaijan every day. One should not be silent about such things,' she was the only Eurovision contestant to meet local human rights activists while she was in the country's capital Baku for the Eurovision final which she won. Azerbaijan is also rated the worst country in Europe for LGBT rights, according to the International Lesbian, Gay, Bisexual, Trans and Intersex Association advocacy group ILGA-Europe.

The Azerbaijan government subsequently warned against politicising the contest and asked the European Broadcasting Union to prevent such meetings. But, adamant that no competition rules had been broken, the organisers took no action against Loreen and the Swedish delegation.

'Azerbaijan was tense,' Loreen recalled during an interview with *Rolling Stone* magazine. 'The dictator [Ilham Aliyev, who's been in power since 2003] was so annoyed by me,' she laughed. 'My security said, "We think you should stay in the hotel", because [Aliyev] was very annoyed by me doing all these things. Me and my producer, we celebrated. All of us in the delegation just said, "Is he annoyed? Cheers!"'

She followed the Baku trip up with a visit to Belarus, where she met the wife of an imprisoned pro-democracy activist. Her enhanced profile meant that she also had a chance to put the spotlight on girls' education in Afghanistan. She became an ambassador of the Swedish Committee for Afghanistan (SCA) and visited Kabul and the village Yaskin Bala in Warsaj Valley with Carl Bildt, Sweden's foreign minister.

Having kept up her interest in humanitarian projects ever since, Loreen says 'yes' to as many opportunities as possible and focuses particularly on women's issues and human and LGBTQ+ rights.

As she said in her documentary *Livet enligt Loreen*, 'You get, you give… I have to give because I get so much. One is aware of the balance'. She went on to say that she ignored all comments from record companies who told her that she couldn't mix charity with her music.

In March 2022, Loreen performed at *Sverige samlas och hjälper*, a live fundraising gala in Sweden in support of Ukraine following the Russian invasion and subsequent war.

At the 2022 Eurovision Loreen said she was supporting the ultimately victorious Ukrainian entry, *Stefania*, by Kalush Orchestra. 'I know some people don't want to mash up human rights with creativity, but I think they go hand in hand. I knew [winning] would mean so much for the Ukrainians and give them strength, because they're in a really dark place.'

'To me creativity without purpose is not interesting enough to me. I can't create without knowing why I create'.

Loreen performs at Heaven on April 18, 2023 in London, England

we got the power

i'm in it with you

Ever since winning Eurovision in 2012, Loreen has been an important ally and a vocal supporter of the LGBTQ+ community, actively engaging with their campaigns to promote equality, visibility, and inclusivity.

Her LGBTQ fans adore her music and performances – particularly her many songs which feature themes of self-acceptance and empowerment. To them she is an icon, much appreciated for using her platform to address LGBTQ+ issues, including speaking out against discrimination.

Loreen is an extremely private person as regards her personal life and is always guarded when the subject comes up in interviews. One of her few pronouncements on the matter came years later in early 2017, when headlines declared she was bisexual following an interview on Swedish television. But in fact it was quite a half-hearted 'declaration' because the interviewer Renee Nyberg had asked a question about her love life to which she had answered 'love is where you find it'. The journalist then said, 'So, you're bisexual?' And I said, 'I guess I am, because love is where you find it. Love is love.'

In a subsequent interview with *Attitude* magazine, Loreen said that she had been in love with a girl '...when I was 'a kid. For me at least it's such a natural thing so I didn't give it that much thought, it was so natural'.

Whatever her personal experiences, Loreen is loved and appreciated by the LGBTQ+ community. Her natural affinity with the movement, was further cemented by her participation and success in Eurovision which has long had close links with LGBTQ+ fans and artists. No Pride event these days is complete without a rendition of *Euphoria*. Drag queens love to belt out her songs and she's a frequent headliner at Pride events. She has even earned the accolade of being an LGBTQ+ 'mother' – a term used to recognise an older, caregiving member of the community.

i'm in it with you | 115

Numerology

Loreen's love of all things spiritual extends to the study of numerology. Her number is 11. She noted that when she returned to Eurovision with Tattoo it had been 11 years since her Euphoria win and she also performed at no 11 in her semi-final.

Loreen performs at Pride Barcelona 2023 on July 15, 2023 in Barcelona, Spain

116 | loreen *She's The One*

Loreen likes:

Dogs

Science fiction

Tagine

Nature

Numerology

In 2015 she headlined one of Europe's biggest charity events, the Vienna Life Ball which supports people with HIV and AIDS in Austria.

In 2023 she was named a 'Pride Icon' at the *Attitude* Pride Awards, which celebrate those who have "championed rights or challenged stigma in the face of adversity".

In an interview with *Attitude* magazine about her award, Loreen said; 'This community, they embraced me. They let me be me. They let me be creative. I've never felt more at home than with this community. It's such an important part of me because it's me! I've realised that I don't want to be anyone else.

"These are my people, we have the same mindset. If somebody asked me, "what is it to feel free?" It's just doing what you feel, expressing yourself exactly the way you want to express yourself, loving yourself the way you want to and talking the way you want to talk. When you don't care what people think, that is true freedom. If you compare it to another community where there are rules and regulations on how you're supposed to look and talk, that's a …jail'.

She also told *Pink News* that the LGBTQ+ community had helped her find where she belonged in the world. 'Before *Euphoria*, I was trying to find my space. Where do I belong? Like, where can I be me?' she said. 'I was searching, and wherever I went, there was "no". All of a sudden, I came knocking on this door to the LGBT community, and they're like: "You know what? Come on in".'

"That's the thing with this community, which I would like to call my community. We're accepting of people. We know what it's like struggling trying to find yourself. That's the beauty of struggling sometimes; we feel empathy, we understand.

'Without this community, I would not be sitting here. Whenever I'm in my community, I would say I feel very much at peace.'

loreen *She's The One*

Loreen performs at Pride Barcelona 2023 on July 15, 2023 in Barcelona, Spain

long live queen loreen

With her name now permanently lodged in the pop music history books, the world is clamouring for more from this most distinctive of artists who is proving such a powerful creative force.

Loreen puts her success down to the fact that 'People want truth and to believe that you are authentic.'

'My approach to music might differ a bit compared to many others. I'm a nomad with my roots in the Atlas Mountains, where music and sound are used for the purpose of healing - which I consider is my purpose too. I always ask myself, what can I offer that will move and engage more people to conversations?'

As she referenced, she didn't have the easiest start in life, and it took real grit to become the international phenomenon that she is today.

Certainly Loreen has bowed to nothing and nobody as she has risen to stardom, never hesitating to ruffle feathers and 'tell it how it is' as she does things 'her way'.

It's a lesson Loreen says she learned from her mother. 'She always fed us with a mantra - there are no rules. Don't let anyone take you down. You are worth everything even if you lose.' Speaking to *Vogue* Arabia in 2017 about how her family has influenced her career, she said. "Music is a big part of how my Moroccan family spend time together. Everybody can sing or play an instrument. It's a huge part of the Moroccan tradition. I never strived to be the centre of attention or a public figure as an artist, I just wanted to perform and create. It has such a healing effect on my spirit and is my way of connecting and communicating with people. When I perform, I feel totally in sync with myself.'

Despite her fame she still manages to keep her private life to herself, helped by the fact that she has made her home on the remote Swedish island of Gotland.

But she has always been clear that spirituality is everything to her, underpinning her beliefs, personality and outlook on life. She believes her simple yet spiritual heritage, accounts for her love of nature and meditation. She sets aside time every year to get away and dedicate herself to meditation and self-understanding and she told **Vogue Scandinavia** that this strong connection to her internal energies is what helps her cope with the pressures of life as a 21st century celebrity. 'You know, let's call it mind control. Observing my own thoughts, to see how unpredictable they are.'

Her experiences as a child, along with the personal histories of her mother, grandmother and great-grandmother have influenced her massively. 'I know what suffering feels like', she says. 'If you've been in pain, and allowed yourself to be in pain, or life has given you painful situations, at some point, when you see another person in pain? Ooof, I can feel that, and I know what you're going through, I can imagine what you're going through. That's why you can't stop from reacting.'

She continued to muse on this theme during an interview with **The Guardian** just after her historic second Eurovision win.

'You can be a favourite, and then it'll flip. You're up, you're down. I have a ground rule: I don't want to know what people are saying, I don't want to know the positive, I don't want to know the negative. If they say I suck, of course I'm going to care. If they think I'm the greatest, that's too much pressure. I don't want to go on that rollercoaster.

'My absolute favourite artists are those who dare to challenge, dare to question, who break free and liberate themselves. That's where I want to be…'

Speaking in the **Livet enligt Loreen** documentary, Loreen expanded on her approach to her work, saying, 'In the creative area many have mixed up integrity with the need for control.

long live queen loreen | 121

When it comes to creativity many people don't know that as a child it was my refuge. My approach to my song is connected to the soul and the heart. It's like me. When I create, I use everything that I am. There is no separation really. It has made me have a need to make sure everything is handled properly. Many people see it as a need for control, that I am like a hawk around my creativity, my expression and so on.'

She further acknowledged that she could sometimes get too involved in things and, referencing **Statements** in particular, she said that 'I can get tunnel vision…especially in work, but in everything if I'm not careful. Sometimes I succeed, sometimes I fail. You have to have a lot of ego to be a creator and have vision and goals. If I do not believe in myself then who will?

With her name now so synonymous with Eurovision that she is also known as its 'Queen', millions believe in her and she's likely to make headlines for years to come.

But as she's demonstrated before, she won't rest on those Eurovision laurels and is likely to carry on producing interesting work and collaborations as her style and identity evolves. She will never do exactly what is expected.

long live queen loreen

discography

Singles and Swedish chart positions

2011

My Heart is Refusing Me #9

Sober #26

2012

Euphoria #1

Crying Out Your Name #19

2013

Heal (Promotional single featuring Blanks)

In My Head

We Got the Power #52

2015

Paper Light (Higher) #25

I'm in it with You

Under ytan

2017

Statements #13

2023

Tattoo #1

As featured artist

2004
Vill Ha Dig (with Freestyle) from Det Basta fran Idol 2004 (Best from Idol 2004)

2005
The Snake (with Rob 'n' Raz) Non album single

2013
Requiem Solution (Kleerup featuring Loreen)

2014
Son (with Ingá-Máret Gaup-Juuso)

2016
Get Into It (Boston Bun featuring Loreen)

2017
Body

Jungle ft Elliphant

71 Charger

Hate The Way I Love You

Albums

2012
Heal

2017
Nude (EP)

Ride